Songs of Jerusalem
and Myself

Also by Yehuda Amichai

POETRY

Poems

PROSE

Not of This Time, Not of This Place

Harper & Row, Publishers
New York, Evanston
San Francisco
London

YEHUDA AMICHAI

Songs of Jerusalem and Myself

TRANSLATED FROM THE HEBREW
BY HAROLD SCHIMMEL

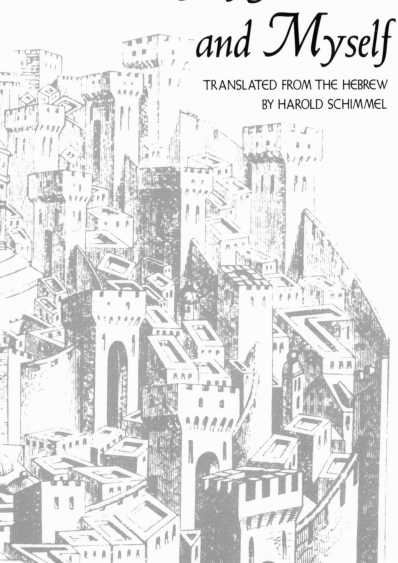

"Evidence," "White Negress," and "In a Foreign Country" first appeared in *Exile*.

Portions of "Jerusalem 1967" first appeared in *Midstream*.

Some of these poems first appeared in *American Poetry Review*.

FIRST EDITION

Designed by Gloria Adelson

Library of Congress Cataloging in Publication Data

Amichai, Yehuda.
Songs of Jerusalem and myself.

    1. Jerusalem—Description—Poetry. 2. Poetry of
places—Jerusalem. I. Schimmel, Harold, tr.
II. Title.
PJ5054. A65S6   892.4'1'6   72–181604
ISBN 0–06–010097–4
ISBN 0–06–010101–6 (pbk)

Contents

Part II

Part 1

Sleep in Jerusalem

While a chosen people
become a nation like all the nations,
building its houses, paving its highways,
breaking open its earth for pipes and water,
we lie inside, in the low house,
late offspring of this old landscape.
The ceiling is vaulted above us with love
and the breath of our mouth
is as it was given us
and as we shall give it back.

Sleep is where there are stones.
In Jerusalem there is sleep. The radio
brings day-tunes from a land
where there is day.
And words that here are bitter,
like last year's almond on a tree,
are sung in a far country, and sweet.

And like a fire
in the hollowed trunk of an olive tree
an eternal heart is burning red
not far from the two sleepers.

Song on Caesarea Beach

I swam far out
beyond the jetty and suddenly stopped moving
like a ship at standstill in deep sea,
the excited passengers not knowing the reason.
It was not from tiredness. The sea was quiet
and my strength was with me. I contemplated the uselessness
of returning. Why should a man return to the shore?
I saw it yellow and gray, not like land
but like a horizon, like the one in the west
that marks with a thin line
the beginning of further distances.
Why return?

Then a beating began inside me
like a muffled engine throbbing in a ship.
This was forgetfulness which began to beat:
an engine far too strong for the needs of my life,
too big for my body, more powerful than all memories
and carrying me far out beyond my death.

God's Hand in the World

1

God's hand in the world
like my mother's
in the guts of the slaughtered hen
on Friday.
What does God see beyond the window
as he puts his hand into the world?
What does my mother see?

2

My pain is already an old man:
it has borne two generations
of pains that resemble it.
My hopes put up white tenements
far from the stress in me.

My girl forgot her love on the sidewalk
like a bicycle. All night out, in the dew.

Children sketch my private history
and the history of Jerusalem
with moon chalk on the road.
God's hand in the world.

Songs to Myself

1

My soul is damaged like the lungs of a diamond cutter.
Beautiful and hard are the days of my life.

My body is like a bank note without cover.
If someone demands gold, I'll have to die.

Already my hands are in their place, my eyes are,
my house is, only I still drift.

I drift.
Beautiful and hard are the days of my life.

2

The world and I have eyes in common:
I look with them into it, it looks into me.

If I weep
the world doesn't care.

But if the world weeps into me
I flood my banks.

3

Like an infant messing itself with food
I want to mess myself with the world's problems.

All over my face, my eyebrows,

my shirt, my trousers, the tablecloth.

The dress of my love, my mother,

the mountains and the sky, all the people,
the feet of angels.

Cradle Song

Sleep, my son, sleep.
The song is not a song
and the cradle's not a cradle.
I'm not at hand,
but the distance will draw us off—
me there and you here. Sleep,

my son, sleep.
In my heart there aren't even
wild flowers like
in the empty lot
after the rains.
But words I have in my mouth,
for your sleep, words.

Sleep, my son, sleep.
The orange peels
will resurrect
and be an orange
from your dreams, my son,
and Trumpledor* will find again
his arm. Sleep.

Sleep, my son, sleep,
free of all your clothes.
In the mosque they take off shoes,

*Trumpledor: an almost legendary one-armed hero of the Jewish settlement in Palestine.

8

in the synagogue wear a hat,
in church remove.
You're free of all that—
sleep, my son, sleep.

I Am Big and Fat

I am big and fat.
Against every ounce of fat
was added an ounce of sadness.

I was a great stutterer, but since
I learned to lie, my speech pours out like water.
Only my face stayed heavy,
like syllables impossible to pronounce,
stumble-stones, stammering.

Sometimes my eyes still show flashes
like fire from remote guns
very far inside me. Old battle.

I demand of others
not to forget. Myself, only to forget.

In the end, forgotten.

The Bull Comes Home

The bull comes home from his workday in the ring
after drinking coffee with his fighters
and leaving them a note with his exact address
and the place of the red handkerchief.
(The sword stays stuck in his stiff-necked neck.
And it stays.)
And he's at home now
and sitting on his bed, with his heavy
Jewish eyes. He knows
it hurts the sword too, when it plunges into flesh.
In the next reincarnation he'll be a sword:
the hurt will stay.
("The door
is open. If not, the key is under the mat.")
He knows the mercy of evening
and true mercy. In the Bible
he is listed with the clean animals.
He is very kosher, chews his cud,
and even his heart's divided and cleft
like a hoof.
Out through his breast break hairs
dry and gray as from a split mattress.

There Are Many Grapes This Year

There are many grapes this year
but there is no peace in my heart. I eat them
Like a mad bird among scarecrows.

A smell of the last fruit has become
a smell of wine
that no one drinks. Big, black
grapes have turned my mouth
into a woman's insides.
Your lips discovered a ripe fig;
they'll stay that way through winter.
People interpreted bright landscapes
of summer's end, but I was thinking
about my love, which will not suffice
to cover this big land.

It has been a long year, filled
with fruit and the dead.
We wait for rain more than ever.
There are many grapes this year; the last are
yellow like the color of wild wasps
which are their death from within.

Resurrection

Afterward they'll get up
all at once, and with a sound of moving chairs
face the narrow exit.

And their clothes are wrinkled
and clods of soil and cigarette ash
are scattered over them
and fingers will uncover in an inside pocket
a theater ticket from a long-gone season.

And their faces still show the crisscross
of God's inclinations.
And their eyes are red from so much sleeplessness
underground.

And immediately—questions:
What time is it?
Where did you put mine?
When? When?

One with an antique upturned face
seems looking— Are there clouds?
Or someone
with a very ancient gesture wipes her eyes
and lifts the heavy hair
at her nape.

Flags

Flags
make the wind.
The wind doesn't
make the wind.

The earth makes
our death.
Not us.

Your face turned west
makes the wandering in me,
not my feet. The roads don't
make the wandering in me,
not Abel's murder,
your face does.

Games

Yes. Drop the words on the table
in a crazy heap
in this Japanese game
of delicate sticks.
Take one
without moving the others.
It moved! It moved!

Or another game: warm,
cold, very cold, a little warmer,
very warm, burning . . . cold.
Afterward, she licks
her lips with a pointed tongue,
then, passing a fingertip lightly over them,
closes like an envelope.

Signs and Testimonies
at Gan Haim Grove

1

Face (woman's)
face, sand face between
rows of dark trees, like tracks
of a heavy wheel that passed.
Imprint of a woman's face.

And an abandoned shoe
filled with sky.
Don't be afraid: no more
will it be filled with a foot.
It won't go.
Just one shoe.

2

Which cloud? The one that was. Was
when? Which one?
A table, a teapot, a cloud, all these
in the past now,
like passing verbs.
A few swimming strokes
remembered from last summer.
(Give regards to whom?
From whom?)

Clouds colored themselves gold
and were beautiful, or bamboo cane
creaked in a dream of a long journey.
A woman undressing in a rickety shack.
The combination—well known.

Evidence

1

It was like silver, like certain.
It hurt.

Smell of the yellow flower calling up desert.
They were three. Face of the one
the face of an eagle. The second was called
to a different place
and went.

2

They met among trees.
Cast their love and shadow groundward
and remained standing.
Pointed that way
and said: That way
must be the Dead Sea. That's
where we die.

Behind them were sad animals
one beside the other.

Her thighs were broad and conclusive.
Her head final.

Forehead known.

3

Or evidence of tree on humans:
    Two.
    They sat beneath me,
    they lay down.
    After that I didn't see them.
Deference of the fathers will shield them, or
some other great cloak.

White Negress

Again I long for
strange lighted windows.
Maybe a man, maybe stands, maybe
before a mirror.
Or that white snow falls inside,
a strange king lies
on a woman that might have
been mine.

A white Negress on the Street of the Abyssinians
that has the voice of a daring boy
before it breaks.

When I'll sit with her in a hot bath
I'll hear from the alleys
arguments on religions.

Who Was There?

In these after-night hours:
no longer words,
only longitudes, lines
on a map,
a few numbers.
Not even that.

And here the gate:
I never imagined
loneliness as a gate:
I thought
a wall.

And the call of the guard in me:
Halt!
Who goes there?

Who *was* there?

Suicide Attempts of Jerusalem

Tears, here, don't soften
the eyes. They only polish
the hardness of faces, like rock.

Suicide attempts of Jerusalem:
She tried again on the ninth of Ab.*
She tried in red and in fire
and in slow destruction
by wind and white dust.

She'll never succeed;
but she'll try again and again.

*The anniversary of the destruction of the temple.

My Father, My King

My father, my king, groundless love
and groundless hate have formed my face
like the face of this dry land.
The years have made me a taster of pain.
Like a wine-taster I distinguish
between kinds of silence,
and know what is dead. And who.

My father, my king, may my face
be not torn by laughter or weeping.
My father, my king, make all that happens
between lust and sadness
not torment me too much; make all things
I do against my will
seem by my will. And my will
like flowers.

I've Been Invited to Life

I've been invited to life. But
I see my hosts showing signs
of weariness and impatience.
Trees stir, clouds become
more and more silent, hills shift
from place to place, the sky is yawning.
And in the nights winds move
things uneasily: smoke, people, lights.

I sign the guest book
of God: I was here, I stayed on,
I loved it, it was great, I was guilty, I betrayed.
I was much impressed by the warm welcome
in this world.

Our Love Has Reached Its End

Our love has reached its end.
Time's defense lines are broken,
brave lies fall one by one.

My city, Jerusalem, is a stage
on which I appear from time to time
in a tragic pose.
She remembers similar ones
from Jeremiah
with his "My intestines! My intestines!"—
a crazy bagpipe,
a sensitive land mine of weeping and wailing.

Our love has reached its end.
And soon the old blunt knives
will be out,
for a new encounter of pain and show.

Darwin's Theory

I speak in the name of those
who according to Darwin's theory should have
died and vanished generations ago. I'm
one of them. My genitals swell in a last flowering,
instruments of my fruits and my love. My bones,
which have supported my life and served it faithfully,
turn, slowly, into final implements,
installations of my end.

The weakness which takes hold of my memory
to remember my son and Jerusalem is the same weakness
which is in my knees and my neck.
The same pain. The same peace.

On a Plane

1

I direct the jet
of cool air
to my temple. Afterward
to between my legs.
Like a radiant beam of the early saints.

The plane thinks it is
a passenger plane,
but it is a bomber:
I'm a bomb.

2

I tour the world
in death throes.
Reflexes of fear and hope
move me from country
to country.

Besides great weariness
I have nothing in common with the sea
down there. Weariness
to be what it is,
what I am.

Aunt Amalia Died

Aunt Amalia died in the quiet of her days.
Last of my father's sisters,
his last echo
in this world.

When I, in calm despair, scratch
at the nape of my neck, I feel its hardness.
That comforts me a little.

Her life was never so good
or bad I'd have
to swear by it, falsely.

In the history of my love she has no chapter.
But I'll have to take
her eternity into consideration.

Aunt Amalia died.
Last of my father's seven sisters,
his last face here.

Love in a Season of Truth

What grows,
what thinks
in this spring?

What of the night? You, you of the night—
a signaling of you.

And the voice what? Blood
in the channels of your transparent body
(you hear it).

Washing hands, cutting fingernails.
Yell. Rough combing without water.
Hurts.
("What do you want from me?")

And telling the truth.
Yes, yes, be fruitful and multiply!
Yes, yes.

Just As It Was

Just as it was.
When the water we drank in the nights, afterward,
was all the wine in the world.

And doors, I'll never remember
whether they open in or out,
switches at the entrance to your house
to turn on lights, for ringing or silence.

We wanted it that way. Is that the way we wanted it?
In our three rooms,
by the open window,
you promised me there would be no war.

I gave you a watch instead of
a wedding ring: good and round time,
the ripest fruit
of sleeplessness and forever.

Last Your Hair Dried

Last your hair dried.
When we were already far from the sea,
when words and salt, which mixed on us,
separated from each other
with a sigh,
and your body no longer showed
signs of terrible antecedents.
In vain we forgot a few things on the beach,
as a pretext to return.
We did not return.

And these days I remember the days
on which your name was fixed like a name on a ship.
And how we saw, through two open doors,
a man thinking, and how we looked
at the clouds with the ancient look
we inherited from our fathers
waiting for rain,
and how at night, when the world had cooled,
your body held on to its heat a long time
like a sea.

We Did It

We did it in front of the mirror
and in the light. We did it in darkness,
in water and in the high grass.

We did it in honor of man
and in honor of beast and in honor of God.
But they didn't want to know about us,
they'd already seen our sort.

We did it with imagination and colors,
with confusion of reddish hair and brown
and with difficult gladdening
exercises. We did it
like wheels and holy creatures
and with chariot feats of prophets.
We did it six wings
and six legs.

But the heavens
were hard above us
like the earth of the summer beneath.

During Our Love Houses Were Completed

During our love houses were completed
and someone, beginning then,
learned to play the flute. His études
rise and fall. You can hear them
now when we no longer fill each other
as birds fill a tree,
and you change coins, compulsively,
from country to country,
from urge to urge.

And even though we acted madly,
now it seems we didn't swerve much
from the norm, didn't distrub
the world, its people and their sleep.
But now it's over.

Soon
of us two there won't be left either
to forget the other.

You Return

You return, not of your own will,
like the sea by its laws.
The waters of Greece and Cyprus on your lips.
The waters of Brindisi
drying in your hair, at my side,
in this sand
whose last memory is the last wave.

Here death is not
that deep: "You can
stand in it."

Salt in the sky, peace in my heart.
These are days of quiet
and of joined branches on the beach.
Birds descended to the water.
"In this season they get mixed up
sometimes and come to a place
they have not come to."

In Front of the Concrete Wall

In front of the concrete wall
I saw you
lit by the last sun, and beautiful
with first doubts.

On the roof, clothes hung up to dry
were forgotten.
Clothes that had your body's shape.

And like a man who enters
another's words,
other seasons
entered us
and did not let us finish.

Love on a Friday Afternoon

A braided challah, you and me
with sabbath-love.

In the room I blacken your skin
with fresh newspaper fingers.

You hear a tune in your ears
and in them still
the leftover murmuring of my lust,
like in an ashtray.

The sun's too much for you:
you'll put dark glasses
on your eyes.

The world will see you
darker than me.

Navel

In our time there are no longer
declarations of war—
there is war.
And there are no declarations of love.

In a light nightgown
split to the chin, you stood up against me.
One word
(the madwoman laughed in the other room),
one deeply sunk word:
navel.

In the Morning

In the morning I stand near your bed.
My shadow falls on your face
deepens your sleep
adding a little more night.

Like fingers of a smoker
your soul is stained—
addicted to love.

I love you
with all my being, with all my
still being here.

I Sat in Happiness

Your eyes suffered great cold
and great heat
like beautiful glass
and stayed lucid.

I sat in happiness. Like
the straps of a knapsack,
love cut deep into my heart's shoulder.

Your eyes enforced
a new biography.

I sat in happiness. And from now on
I'll be just one side
in the dictionary,
the said or the explained.

Your eyes count and count.

Love Gifts

I gave you, for
your earlobes, for your fingers,
I gilded the time on your wrist,
I hung many shining things on you
so that you'd move in the wind
for me, chime softly over my head,
to soothe my sleep.

I stuffed your bed with apples
(as it is written in the Song of Songs)
so we'd roll smoothly
on a red, apple-bearing bed.

I covered your skin with delicate, pink fabric
transparent as baby lizards
which have eyes of black diamonds in summer nights.

You enabled me to live for a few months
without needing a religion
or a *Weltanschauung*.

You gave me a letter opener of silver:
letters like these aren't opened like that. They're
torn, torn, torn open.

The Last One

The last one
who doesn't run
in a sudden shower
but walks slowly
as before
is first for love,
earmarked
for later.
He'll arrive,
hair
stuck to his forehead
with a smell
of drying wool,
and will love.

Threading

Loving each other
started like that: threading
loneliness into loneliness
with patience
and trembling, exact fingers.

Longing for the past
colored our eyes with a double assurance
of what will never change
and one can never return to.

Yet—one of us
the heart must kill
on one of its skirmishes
(if not you, me)
when it returns empty-handed,
like Cain, a boomerang
from the fields.

Avigayil—Not the Biblical One

Traveled
after the disappointment in love
turned into
a carrier pigeon, light of wing,
and on her right foot the bikini
ring that rolled
to her ankle. (Also
an amulet.)

She stops becoming
and turns into
a superstition,
like a black cat
or a hand with outstretched fingers
or a certain number
or a luminous sky-blue color.

Her desires come out
every hour exactly
like a cuckoo clock.

Try to love her
at exactly twelve o'clock
(in the afternoon or midnight).

Toward the Seventies

A man died whose last name
was like the name of the city
where I was born.
Thus my childhood dies
again and again.

I live now in Jerusalem.
I live, live, live
with quiet stubbornness.

Toward the seventies, decade of blazes.
I gather memories like dry twigs,
thorn and thistle.

Yet I was born in the gay and flaming twenties.
Only once, on a Passover night,
was I sick and very quiet.

My soul—
the folds remained
like in an old letter
I never dared unfold again.

Here.
Yes.
From here
the tearing begins.

My Friend's Father

I saw my friend's father.
Now he no longer speaks aloud
to himself in the street.
A public servant, retired, in twilight.

Compared to him Buber is an eternal student,
arguing on with sweet indulgence.
And Herzl too, leaning on a ship's railing,
his innocent beard streaming in warm dialogue.

"This life is a constant departure
from houses."
The sum of all the stairs
I have already descended
would lift me clear
to heaven.

He Who Relies on Time

He who relies on time
to heal will lose both time and healing.
Time will go by, healing won't come.

He'll set up a draftsman's desk
for his thoughts—
angles and many rulers—
and a weeping lamp bends over him.

Joy and festival will reach
him stammering
like some heavy drink from a dark bottle.

He cannot stay:
the earth already knows too much
about him, even
before he's laid in.

The Death of A.G.

Half an hour ago
my crying stopped.
It's strange and quiet now,
like a factory at evening.

I want to make propaganda
for your death.
I sift your letters
from the others
set apart for life—not so long,
and maybe not better.
I pull the sky down close to my eyes
like someone nearsighted,
to read.

I can't understand your death in London
in the mist,
as I can't understand
my life, here in the bright light.

Bitter Lemon

Bitter lemon, what do you want
from me? I want you to suck me
devour me be bitter with me
and die with me. Sweet mouth,
red mouth's what I want.

Bitter lemon, after that what,
what will we say to them? You're no
honeydew, you're no
honeymoon lodge for my night. You're much, much more.
My mouth will die in you
red, and with my mouth—my rage.

When a Man Changes

When a man changes, he'll always
be a loser—even those not dead
will die—and his belongings will be shifted
from place to place without resurrection.

When a man changes, his son will ask:
"Who slept here last night?"
His tears will flow inside and never dry,
his flesh will wander before the
wandering of his bones, and his sleep
will be scattered in many and far countries.

When a man changes, you can't see his face.
He is like God: he hasn't the
semblance of a body. And those who knew him
will pass through him. He's less than a
mirror, less than a window.

He'll sign letters, unread,
and let his photos develop forever, he'll order
shoes and not take them, and he'll forget
his coat in the wardrobes of strangers.

He'll leave them his dead body
so at least they'll
learn something about him.

Grown Up

They tapped me on the back
as for a child perplexed
in swallowing. They hit me still
and I'm grown up and swallow quietly.
I've learned to read their worthy
penmanship, and also my enemies' script.

Reading music was harder
still, and now I must discern
and read the eyes of those I meet.
And *prove* myself as by Pythagoras'
theorem: I build about me squares and planes
to prove what I really want
and to remain alone in the midst.

My Father's Memorial Day

When the moon is full,
it will be my father's memorial day.
It's always so.

The day of his death will never fall
in summer or in spring.

I put little stones on his tomb:
a sign I was here,
the calling card of one alive
on the big stone of my father. My father,
causer and affected,
your alarm clock breaks my body.

Two sabbath candles of my mother
travel gently side by side in the street,
towed by a ship, not seen.

From a gym hall the hollow echo
of high screams,
vapor and queer sweat
with a smell of girls' thighs and wet rubber.

Father, I now like to wash and comb my hair.
Aside from this, I haven't changed.

The scant information on your tombstone
is less than a passport.

There's no police to tell
I'm a murderer.

When I get home I'll lie down,
arms spread as if crucified.

It calms me,
Father.

Jerusalem 1967

1

This year I traveled far
to view the quiet of my city.
Rocking soothes a baby, distance soothes a city.
I lived in my longing. I played a game
of four severe squares of Yehuda Halevi:
my heart—   my self,   the east,   the west.

I heard bells ringing in time's religions,
but the howl I heard within
is still from my Judean Desert.

Now that I'm back, I cry again.
At night the stars come up like bubbles from the drowned.
Each morning I cry the scream of a newborn baby
From the blind chaos of houses and all this great light.

2

Light against the Tower of David, light
on the Church of Maria, light on the Fathers
asleep in their double graves, light on your face
from within, light on the transparent honey
cakes, light on the clock face, and time
is lighted passing between your thighs
when you take off your dress.

Lighted the round cheeks of my childhood,
lighted the stones that wished to be

lighted, with those that wished to
sleep in the darkness of squares.

Lighted the spiders of railings, and
cobwebs of churches and acrobats of
spiral stairs. But of all these, most
is lighted the true and terrible X ray
in letters of white bones and lightning:
Mene   Mene   Tekel   Upharsin.

3

In vain you'll look for barbed-wire fences.
You know such things
don't disappear. Another city, perhaps,
is now cut in two: two lovers
separated; other flesh tormented
by these thorns, refusing to be stone.

In vain you'll look. You lift your eyes unto the hills.
Perhaps there? Not these hills, accidents of geology,
but The Hills. You ask
without raising the voice, without question mark,
to do your part in asking questions
gone now. But a great weariness wants you with all your heart
and gets you. Like death.

Jersualem, the only place in the world
where even the dead have a right to vote.

54

4

It's not time that takes me from my childhood,
but this city and everything in it. Now
to have to learn Arabic, to reach Jericho
from both sides of time; and length of walls
added to height of towers and domes
vast without limit. All these
widen my life and force me
to migrate anew from the smell
of rivers and forest.

My life's stretched out; thinning like cloth,
transparent. You can see through me.

5

The city plays hide-and-seek between names:
Jerusalem, El-Kuds, Shalem, Jeru, Yeru,
whispering: Y'vus, Y'vus, Y'vus, in darkness.
Weeping with longing: Aelia Capitolina, Aelia, Aelia.
She comes to all who call her
at night, alone. But we know
who comes to whom.

6

Jerusalem stone is the only stone
that hurts. It has a network of nerves.
From time to time Jersualem gathers

to mass protest like the tower of Babel.
But with big clubs God-The-Police beats
her back: houses razed, walls torn down,
and then once more the city disperses, midst jabbering
prayers complaint and random cries from churches
and synagogues and minaret shout from mosques.
Each one to his place.

7

I and Jerusalem like blind man and cripple.
She sees for me
until the Dead Sea, until the end of days.
And I hoist her on my shoulders
and walk blind in my darkness beneath.

8

On this clear autumn day
I build Jerusalem anew.
Foundation scrolls
fly in the air, birds, thoughts.

God is angry with me
because I force him, always,
to create the world from Beginning:
Chaos, Light, Second Day, to
Man and back again.

9

In the morning the shadow of the Old City falls
on the New. In the afternoon, the reverse.
Nobody profits. The muezzin's prayer
is wasted on the new houses. The ringing
of bells rolls like a ball, and rebounds. Seraphic
praise from synagogues will fade like gray smoke.

At the end of summer I breathe this air,
the parched and aching. A silence
like many shut books is thought:
many closed books, most of whose pages are
stuck like eyelids in the morning.

10

I go up David's Tower,
a little above the most exalted prayer,
halfway to heaven. Some
of the ancients succeeded: Muhammad, Jesus
and others. But didn't find rest in heaven;
they entered a higher excitement. But
the applause for them hasn't let up
below.

11

Jerusalem is built on vaulted foundations
of a held-back shout. Without a reason

for the shout, the foundations would give, the city would
    totter;
if the shout is shouted, Jerusalem would explode skyward.

12

Poets come with evening into the Old City
and leave it loaded with images
and metaphors and little maxims
and twilight similes between vaults and rims.
Darkening fruits
and wrought-iron filigree of the heart.

I lifted my hand to my forehead
to wipe the sweat
and brought up Else Lasker-Schüler
by chance. Light and small as she was in her life,
how much more so in her death. But her poems!

13

Jerusalem port city on the shores of eternity.
The Holy Mount is a huge ship, a luxurious pleasure
liner. From the portholes of her Western Wall happy
saints look out, travelers. Hasidim on the dock wave
good-bye, shout hurrah till we meet again. She's
always arriving, always sailing. And the gates and the docks
and the policemen and the flags and the high masts of
    churches

and mosques and the smokestacks of synagogues and the
    boats
of praise and waves of mountains. The sound of the ram's horn
    is heard: still
another sailed. Day of Atonement sailors in white uniforms
climb among ladders and ropes of seasoned prayers.

And the trade and the gates and the gold domes:
Jerusalem is the Venice of God.

Part 2

Spy

Many years ago
I was sent
to spy out the land
beyond the age of thirty.

And I stayed there
and didn't go back to my senders,
so as not to be made
to tell
about this land

and made
to lie.

End of Summer Evening in Motsa

A lone bulldozer fights with his hill
like a poet, like all who work here alone.
A heavy lust of ripe figs
pulls the evening's ceiling to the level of the earth.
Fire has already eaten the thorns
and death won't have to do a thing except
fold up like disappointed flames.
I can be consoled: a great love
can also be a love for landscape.
A deep love for wells, a burning for olive trees,
or digging like bulldozers alone.

My thoughts are always polishing my childhood
till it's become like a hard diamond,
unbreakable, to cut
into the cheap glass of my maturity.

Hike with a Woman

When after hours of walking
you discover suddenly
that the body of the woman stepping beside you
wasn't meant
for travel and war,

and that her thighs have become heavy
and her buttocks move like a tired flock,
you swell with a great joy
for the world
in which women are like that.

The Death of Celan

I heard about it in London.
They said he killed himself.

The same rope
was tugging lightly at my neck.
But it wasn't a rope: he
died by water.
The same water, water, water.

Last metaphor:
a life like a death.
(The same water, water, water.)

Psalm

A song on a day
some building contractor
cheated me. A psalm.
Plaster falls from the ceiling,
the wall is sick, paint cracks like lips.

The vines I've sat under, the fig tree,
all are words. The rustling of leaves
gives an illusion of God and of justice.

I dip my dry look
like bread into the softening death
that is always on the table before me.
Already my life has turned
my life into a revolving door.
I think of those who, in happiness and success,
have left me behind, those
who like pampered and brilliant grapes
are carried for show between two
and those who are also carried
between two and they are wounded or dead. A psalm.

When I was a child I sang in the synagogue choir,
I sang until my voice broke. I sang
first voice and second voice. I'll sing
until my heart breaks, first heart and second heart.
A psalm.

My Portion

Your eyes quiet as mouths.
Your mouth like under the surface of water.
Your face like sand shifting.

Thus you gathered your hair
you gathered the days and the words
in what other times would call
a home.

"Never again"—never
is also eternity,
my taste of eternity,
my portion in it.

These Are Preparations for a Journey

These are preparations for a journey. You open
the window. (Don't close it! the air is changing.) A dry
leaf on the bed. I begin to long
for things that are with me, as if they were not.
Preparations for a journey. No eating. No walking.
No standing together. And each night distances
are filled into people like milk
into bottles outside their door. These are preparations
for a journey. My father was trapped inside the holy ark.
The night after Simchat Torah,* shut with all the glittering
scrolls in the dark. He weeps softly, the way he never
wept in his life. He speaks, muffled, with *his* voice
and my son's. Calls me "my father" and "my son" alternately.
The hammering of his fists from within
stays with me always. These are preparations for a journey.

Man was created to walk upright, on two,
but sometimes his soul wants to stretch out on all four
and lie inside him, only this. Preparations for a journey.

---

*Feast of the Law.

In a Foreign Country

In a foreign country you must love
a girl who is a history student.
You lie with her in this grass
at the foot of these hills
and between yells and groans
she'll tell you
what happened here in the past.
"Love is a serious matter": I
never saw animals laughing.

Instructions for a Waitress

Don't remove the glasses and plates
from the table. Don't rub
the stain from the cloth. It's good to know:
people were here before me.

I buy shoes which were on another man's feet.
(My friend has thoughts of his own.)
My love is another man's wife.
My night is "used" with dreams.
On my window raindrops are painted,
in the margins of my books are notes by others.
On the plan of the house in which I want to live
the architect has drawn strangers near the entrance.
On my bed is a pillow, with
a hollow of a head now gone.

Tourist in Jerusalem

Refreshing girl
like Jericho oranges with leaves
attached so you're convinced
they're fresh.

A girl is such with her dreams
from her green country,
so they'll believe her.

And my love is carved
as
from olive wood. As for tourists.

Night* with an Armenian suffix:
Le-li-an.
Clear like the white in the eye at night
Ai, tallow, tallow.

*Lai-la, in Hebrew.

Damascus Gate in Jerusalem

I forget how the road was
a month ago, but I remember it
from the Crusader era, for example.

(Excuse me, this fell. Is it yours?
The stone? Not this, this fell
nine hundred years ago.)

A great gate and at its feet
a little whelp gate.
A blind old man bends to tie
the shoe of his baby grandchild.

(Excuse me, where can I find the Public
Forgetter?)

A childhood grown old is my maturity:
Fever of my days, "shower of all my days," said
Dylan, who is flood tide.

"In the courtyards of our Lord they'll flourish." What are
those courtyards? Like what?

Medlar

I always forget to ask
if it's allowed to eat
the medlar fruit, if it's forbidden.
This name might well have been
a woman's name
of the proudest, that live only once.

I'm a lonely man,
and at the terrible weddings
I've broken more glass than bridegrooms.

My eyes to the waterfall of words
within.
My dark blood—
my true coat.

Poem on the Renovation of My House

With eyes that have seen the gold of Kuwait
and the black cream of oil,
Taleb is at work reconstructing my house
for several thousand pounds
which he changes into dinars; then
to the gold within his eyeballs.

He raises my roof that fell in.
Like an elegant tennis player he flicks plaster
on the walls of my room, and so changes
my biography.

Coiled springs under his feet, he passes
through the Old City after work.
A sweet, meandering and twisting river
in deep and blue charm,
like ribbons in long hair. Taleb
sees a stranger covered with golden down
all over her body: a hairy alien beast
making shadows dance in the alleys. He sees
a policeman riding a white horse,
wings of a parachuted angel on his chest.

Blessed is summer,
the grass on the slope is burnt.
Burning, too, is a language.

With All the Severity of Compassion

Count them.
You may count them. They
are not like the sand on the shore. They
are not like the boundless stars.
They are like lonely people
at the corner, and on the street.

Count them. See them
seeing your heaven through ruined houses.
Come out from the stones and
go back. Where? But count them
because they spur their days with dreams
yet walk free, and their hopes,
which are not tended, are open wounds.
They will die of them.

Count them.
Too early, they learned to read the terrible
writing on the wall. To read and write
on other walls,
while the feast goes on in silence.

Count them. Be present;
they have already used all the blood, and
are still short, as in a dangerous operation,
when one is tired and defeated
like ten thousand. For who judges
and what is judgment
if not with the full meaning of night
and with all the severity of compassion.

Too Many

Too many olive trees in the valley.
Too many stones on the hill's slope.
Too many dead, too little
earth to cover them all.
And I must return to the landscapes painted
on bank notes
and to my father's face on coins.

Too many remembrance days, too little
remembering. My friends have forgotten
what they learned in their youth.
And at a hidden place my love lies
and I am always outside,
food for the hungry winds.
Too much tiredness, too few eyes
to hold it. Too many clocks,
too little time. Too many oaths
on the Bible. Too many roads, too few
ways for a man to really go:
to his destiny.
Too many hopes
that fled their masters.
Too many dreamers. Too few dreams
whose solution would change
the history of the world
like Pharaoh's dreams.

My life closes behind me.
And I am outside, a dog

for the cruel and blind wind
pushing always at my back.
I am trained: rise and sit,
waiting to lead him through the streets
that might have been my real life.

Advanced Training for Angels

After the training on round targets
(my life is round like them,
with the black bull's-eye of my childhood
in the center, where I'm vulnerable),
after the training on round targets,
training with dummy men: a head
like a head. A man fleeing.
Or people passing slowly:
a child playing, a man seated in his chair,
my love, at her window,
all passing slowly before the riflemen
on the hill of the broken red
tiles at the edge of the world.

It's Terrible to Identify

It's terrible to identify the dead
after an earthquake, or after a battle.
But it's more terrible to identify them
when they are alive and walking.
Or at seven in the evening
up the street.
When forgetting is gone
but remembrance won't come in its place.

Eternity colors itself with eternity,
water dies in water
and rises from water,
clouds move only among clouds.
Not so with men:
they have to move
among iron and stone,
among all that does not love them.

I had an uncle in whose body
iron from the first World War
remained scattered
till after the second.
When he died, they separated again:
from the iron they made more shells,
from my uncle new uncles,
a new forgetting.

Sort of Apocalypse

The man under his fig tree telephoned the man under his vine:
"Tonight they definitely might come.
Armor-plate the leaves. Secure the tree.
Call the dead home, and make ready!"

The white lamb said to the wolf:
"The human race bleats and my heart aches.
No doubt there'll be close combat there.
At our next meeting we'll discuss it."

All the Nations (united) will stream into Jerusalem
to see if the Law went forth from Zion, and meanwhile

seeing it's now spring
they'll pick flowers,

and beat sword into plowshare and plowshare into sword
then back again, and again and again, without stopping.

Maybe, from so much beating and grinding,
the iron of war will die out.

Half the People in the World

Half the people in the world
love the other half.
Half the people
hate the other.
Must I because of them and of them
go, and wander, and endlessly change
like rain in its cycle, and sleep among rocks, and be rough like
    olive trunks,
and hear the moon bark at me,
and camouflage my love with worries,
and grow like the wavering grass
between the railroad tracks,
and live in the earth like a mole,
and be with roots and not with branches,
and without my cheek on angel's cheek,
and make love in the first cave
and marry my wife under the canopy
of beams which holds up earth,
and play out my death, always
to the last breath and the last
words without understanding,
and set up flagpoles above my house
and a shelter beneath it. And go out
upon the roads made only for return and pass
all the terrible stations—
cat, stick, fire, water, slaughterer,
between the kid and the angel of death?

Half the people love,
half hate.
And where is my place between
the so well-matching halves,
and through what crack will I see the
housing projects of my dreams,
and the barefoot runners on the sands,
or at least the wave
of the girl's handkerchief, by the hill?

All the Generations Before Me

All the generations before me
donated me, bit by bit, so that I'd be
erected all at once
here in Jerusalem, like a house of prayer
or charitable institution.
It binds. My name's
my donors' name.
It binds.

I'm approaching the age
of my father's death. My last
will's patched with many patches.
I have to change my life and death
daily to fulfill all the prophecies
prophesied for me. So they're not lies.
It binds.

I've passed forty.
There are jobs I cannot get
because of this. Were I in Auschwitz
they would not have sent me out to work,
but gassed me straightaway.
It binds.

I Am a Man Alone. I Am Not a Democracy*

I am a man approaching his end.
What seems like youthfulness in me is not
youthfulness, but madness,
because only death can halt this madness.
And what seems like deep roots I put down
is nothing but entanglement on
the surface: spastic knots and cramp of grasping hands,
jumbled ropes and mania of chains.

I am a man alone. I am not a democracy.
The executive, the loving and the legislative power
in one body. The eating, gluttonous, and the vomiting power,
the hating power and power of hurting,
blind power and mute power.
I was not elected. I am a demonstration, I carry
my face like a slogan. It's all written there. Everything.
Please, no need to use tear gas,
I already weep. No need to disperse me,
I am dispersed,
and the dead, too, are a demonstration.
When I visit my father's grave, I see
the tombstones carried high in the hands
of the dust beneath:
they're a mass demonstration.

*This is part of a long autobiographical poem, "The Journey of the Last
Benjamin of Tudela."

85

I think of forgetting as of a slowly ripening fruit,
which once ripe will never be eaten, because it won't be
and won't be remembered:
its ripeness is its forgetting. When I lie
on my back my bones fill
with a sweetness
of my little son's breath.
He breathes the same air as I,
sees the same sights,
yet my breath is bitter and his breath is sweet
like rest in the bones of the tired.
The memory of my childhood be blessed: his childhood.

Jews in the Land of Israel

We forget where we came from. Our Jewish
names from the exile reveal us,
bring up the memory of flower and fruit, medieval cities,
metals, knights that became stone, roses mostly,
spices whose smells dispersed, precious stones, much red,
trades gone from the world.
(The hands, gone too.)

The circumcision does it to us,
as in the Bible story of Shechem and the sons of Jacob,
with pain all our life.

What are we doing here on our return with this pain?
The longings dried up with the swampland,
the desert flowers for us and our children are lovely.
Even fragments of ships, that sunk on the way,
reached this shore,
even winds reached. Not all the sails.

What are we doing
in this dark land that casts
yellow shadows, cutting at the eyes?
(Sometimes, one says even after forty
years or fifty: "The sun is killing me.")
What are we doing with souls of mist, with the names,
with forest eyes, with our lovely children, with swift blood?

Spilled blood isn't roots of trees,
but it's the closest to them
that man has.

A Song of Praise to the Lovely Couple
Varda and Schimmel

Jerusalem in the week of the marriage of
Schimmel: I saw a foreign beatnik shoulder
his wrapped guitar like a rifle.
I saw a beggar put out a jingling hand
at the entrance to the public pissoir across from
buttoning men. And in the Russian compound
I heard at night fresh whores
who sang and danced in jail:
Esty, Esty, Esty, take me.

Jerusalem sunk in audiovisual love,
Jerusalem still drunk,
froth of tourists on her lips.

I take her temperature:
thirty-eight degrees in the shade of her armpits.
one hundred degrees of joy
in the mouth of the gold ring.*

But Motza!†
Schimmel is preparing Motza for his marriage.
From the east seven red bulldozers
cut the mountain like a great wedding cake.
Ten yellow cement mixers, thirty workers
with flags and undershirts of phosphorescent orange.

*Asshole, in Hebrew.
†Motza is a village situated on a mountain not far from Jerusalem.

Twenty-one explosions in the afternoon:
Mazel tov!

Schimmel and Varda are already descending slowly
in the parachute of the white synagogue.
Now they're standing silent, wrapped
in the cellophane paper of God's mercy.

Love in one clean room,
like a dream of years of good living
compressed in one minute of sleep.
Schimmel and Varda:

two tranquilizer pills
melting slowly
in the mouth of the excited and crumbling world.

Achziv Poems*

1

Broken by the sea,
my head a broken tin.
Sea water fills it
and drains out.

Broken by the sea.
A dirge my lament,
froth on the lips of the cliffs.
The sea has rabies,
has sea sickness,
more dog than dog,
more sea than all seas.

Broken by the sea
my lament.

2

Old millstones separated
and laid out for show
at the two ends of the village.
From great longing
they continue to grind between them
lovers' time.

*Achziv: an old village on the north coast of Israel.

Naked people in the sand talk about
political problems. It's absurd!
Little piles of clothes in the distance.
Birds cry from an island. Pink buttocks
and muscles like sleeping fish. It's
absurd even to ask "What's the time?"
when you're naked. A white stripe on your wrist.
Better, dialogue:
"Di-," she said. "alogue," he said.
Di-, di-, di-, alogue, alogue.

Our friend hid his typewriter
in the broom bush. Camouflaged in the branches.
Tak, tak, di-, di-, di-, alogue.

3

All night you lay awake on your back.
There was another wind
and there was a wind like you.
The light of the moon
threw on the wall
one more lattice.
"The key's under the stone near the gate."
In the morning the outline of your body appeared
marked by cigarette butts
on the floor.

4

Your green eyes were
blue for my brown eyes
after this night.

And wrinkles appeared on the sheets:
no, not from age.

5

Around the dead word "we-loved"
covered over by seaweed in the sand
the curious mob crowded.
And until evening we heard the testimonies
of waves, one by one,
how it happened.

6

Much waves, much eyes,
much affliction, much salt,
much sleep, much deceit,
much sadness, song in the nights, much
shells, much sand, the profane, everything.

The explanation—to go on living.
What is our life: so many centimeters of
distraction and tenderness, meat
between the hard skeleton inside
and the hard air outside.

7

My friend saw horses bathing
in the sea at Akko. He saw them and I feel
them galloping. What did we look for
in the sand that Tuesday and Wednesday,
what did we look for?
With a little breath I put out your right ear.
With a little breath I put out your left ear.
With little breaths on both your ears
I lit your lusts. A great
invasion began within us. Our writhing and
twining bodies were witnesses to the greatness of
the tussle.
In vain.

8

Tie your weeping with a chain
and be inside with me.

In the partly ruined house
the light lives by himself.
From the darkness they make delicate silverware
for the last meal.

My fish mouth mouth
and your fish mouth nipple
are attached at night.

93

After that was a moonlit night
whiter than Atonement Day.
Your weeping burst the chain.
Fled.

9

In the sand we were two-headed Cerberus
with bared teeth. In the afternoon
your one leg was in the east and your second in the west
and I in the middle, leaning on my forelegs,
looking to the sides with suspicion, roaring awfully,
lest they take my prey from me.

Who are you?
A poor Jewish kid from the diaspora,
skullcap on the head. From there. From that time.

All night we're together. No
heavy memories, sticky feelings. Just
muscles, tensing and relaxing.

In another continent of time,
the dead rabbis of my childhood appear,
holding the gravestones high over
their heads.
Bound up in the knot of my life.

My God, my God,
Why have you not forsaken me!?

10

With the daring glance of Columbus
I look out between towels hung
in the window. The sun sets
in a red dress.
Four boats pass from evening
to evening from behind a handkerchief.
Salt in the little salt cellar on the table,
and outside all the salt in the world.

Seven crumpled panties
around your bed, for the seven
days we were here.
Seven withered roses
in seven colors.

11

A one-piece bathing suit:
the big voice of the mob.
A crazy somersault.
The applause of my hand on your body,
wild applause.

The dry element and the
moist in a great longing
destroy each other.

Hesitating veins.
Blue trying to look pink.
I live by your ankles.
My member stands up with solemn ceremony
as if to listen.

I'll leave you beside the sea
until your reddish hair goes green,
until my black briefcase is buried in weeds
like a long-sunk ship.
I'll whip cries out of you,
to make up for all the silences.
Heady revenge.
God.

12

I learned
to relate to your cunt
as to a face.

I speak its former language.
Wrinkled, and made of substance older
than all remembered ages, written on a book.

It relates to us
as distant offspring,
playing.

13

Ach seed, ach streaming semen,
Achziv gold oozes
so, so.

Soon the deserted village
will be a second time deserted
by us. Ach you,
hair brown, skin white,
eyes green; but here,
in Achziv, all the red breaks out
in you: you're one
of thirty-six lurking holy incarnadines.
Moss between your thighs,
redskin,
Esau-
ite.

14

Wind, what a waste of wind
you are. To move sand to sand,

me to you, smell to smell.
Wind, what a waste!

Clouds, what a waste of cloud,
not raining, just shifting
the colors of western Galilee a little
for us.

My life, what a waste of life
you are. Just for these days. Here.

15

Tyrus ladders,* lust ladders,
ladders to the roof of Eli's house. Girls
come down, go up, bearing ropes and mattresses,
long hair and underwear to dry. Washday
cries. Laughing-damp won't dry.
Girls go up, come down the ladder.

We see her soul:
it's black and made of fine embroidered net.
We see her pink subconscious,
with dainty lace on it. We see it,
oh, we see it, we see it.

*Tyrus Ladder—*Sulam Tzur*—the name of the coast in northern Israel below
the Lebanese border, on which Achziv is located.

16

In the abandoned house
live a dwarf tamarisk, mint
and sage. Let's visit them
in the afternoon. We'll sit awhile,
rustle with them and send up scents.

There's a red line on your waist
in memory of the elastic.
It will vanish like a sand ledge with the wave,
then we'll know:
our time is ripe to be here.

17

A last night near the window,
outside and in. Hours pass, seven,
nine, ten.   Eleventh hour:
moonlight
turned our bodies into surgical instruments
hard and gleaming with evil.

Another hour, hours, one, two, three,
five: in the first light of dawn
your body was seen caught in the network
of its nerves, like a sheet
that fell during the night and held,
stuck in the branches of the dead tree
before the window.

18

What's it like to be a woman?
What's it like to feel
vacancy between legs and curiosity
under the skirt, in summer, in wind,
and chutzpa* at the haunches?

A male has to live with that odd sack
between his legs. "Where would you like
me to put it?" asked the tailor,
measuring my pants,
and didn't smile.

What's it like to have a whole voice,
that never broke?
To dress and undress   slitherly
slinkily   caressively
like wearing olive oil,
to anoint the body with lithe fabrics,
a silky something,
a murmuring nothing of peach or mauve?
A male dresses with crude gestures of
buckling and edgy undoing,
angles, bones and stabs in the air,
and the wind's entangled in his eyebrows.

*Chutzpa: unmitigated effrontery or impudence. [Yiddish] —*The Random House Dictionary of the English Language*

100

What's it like to "feel a woman"?
And your body dreams you.
What's it like to love me?

Leavings of a woman on my body,
and signs of the male on yours
augur the hell
which awaits us
and our mutual death.

19

If longings start—longings
to be among these houses near this sea,
we'll already be far from them.

My heart's keeners began
too soon, while I'm still here,
to lament and pluck at my blood and at the sea's sand
and weeds; to beat with fists on cliff,
on sand and on your breasts.

The sea retreats from my face.
My face is the floor of the sea: dry
with cracks and rocks and savage winds.
I grew up like that,
the memories of the soft green sea still on my face.

20

After these days, I still don't know much
about you. The palm remains bent to the east
even with no wind from the west. A white boat
passes parallel to the coast, hard
and clear like God's fingers. The last will
I write in Achziv, in the sand,
is different from the one I wrote in Jerusalem.
Children's voices buried beneath layers
on the hill reach us in this century
at this hour of the afternoon. They haven't
stopped playing.

The white, licked beam will never return
and be in a ship, the milled gravel
can never become a rock. It tears at
my heart, as it tore at the prophets'; with a sharp
tearing pain a man's turned into a prophet.
It's a good landscape for forgetting and prophecy.
From now on we'll look for windows with other
views. We'll wander from window to window,
from arch to arch.

Soon the abandoned ship's anchor will be
decoration for houses and yards. Our hearts too
will be just an amulet,
hung inside in dreams and blood.

The Buenos Aires Poems

1

All the while
I didn't see the sea. Then
once, at night, you told me about it.
I didn't want to hear, so that
Buenos Aires would be
like Jerusalem without a sea.

Dolores they called you,
Susanna
is the name of your friend, "Chica,"
a driver, passing, called out.

We both were lost
by two who never knew each other:

two losses crying
and laughing together in the dark.

2

Deep passageways, galleries, a display window
with serious playthings, like a brown race horse,
an ivory chess set on
a scarlet flame of velvet,
grave and bitter playing cards like bitter
chocolate, tobacco that contracts the lips with dim
gold. A hard pipe,
pale dice that didn't melt,

remoteness of a bullfight, smell of tanned leather.
A sign implores with quiet weeping:
Do not smoke.
Inflammation of street lamps like of the eyes,
a light that once really hurt.

You die, you cross the river of memory
to eternal memory. Deep passageways.

3

Precise instruments,
very precise instruments.

A woman surprised by mild pain,
something had fled from the face inward,
a shadow laugh.

Her father's fathers
wiped out the Indian peoples.
A guilt of birds
that hurt the air in their flight
remained within her.

Precise instruments,
very precise instruments.

4

Born near the sea in a city *del Mar,*
was loved in a small room far from it,
lived on a street named for a man dead and forgotten.
Even the taxi driver didn't know how to find
the old house with the quiet door.
Wore a striped dress and spun between the stripes
in a whirlpool. Lost
also among large and printed flowers.

I kissed her mouth which a foreign language
had shaped. And so I learned.
"Hello, hello," despairing in my language,
"Ola?" amused and sad in hers.

And in my winter is her summer and in my day her night.
And in my country days get longer and in hers shorter
and her eyes are a process for melting gold in brown
and her body's shape is like the shape of the opening
in my life.

5

Remnants of an Argentinian funeral
cross my path. Three, four,
already without flowers. The grave is far,
a very elegant funeral, thoroughly urban,
with made-up eye, clean-shaven cheek

and a black dress close to the thigh,
in the flight from death.

And there is a man who has nothing
to bring to burial
but the memory of one night.

     6

In the hotel. I need two
pillows: one under my head
to prevent memories and one over my eyes
so as not to see what's coming.

In the morning I get out of the bed, in which,
next week, I'll forget my pajamas.
I lather soap on my face
with a brush
made from a single plait of your hair.

Downstairs they set Easter pastries
before me, a whole egg baked
into a sweet cake:
my eyes, too, still closed in sleep.

     7

Words hung in the mouth
like a cigarette that didn't light,

and now a migration of birds
begins in me,
from my cold heart to my warm heart.
These birds don't know
I'm the same man (those
outside know it's the same world).

"In this room
two can be strangers
to each other, as in a huge time."

8

A girl on Avenida Santa Fe. Additional
eyes are drawn on hers, lips
smeared with the white of the beautiful dead,
very long eyelashes, her eye's teeth.

A psychology student: fourth
year of the passing leisure
of knowledge in her convex and pleasant brain.

A small gold cross on her neck
(I come from a country where it's real and heavy)
and both of us are at different stages
in the process of giving in;
despair of "the good" is quiet here.
In my country it gushes blood.

"Far off," she said.
The streets begin far off,
are caught in the city and move again
to sea, to plains, to air.

"Anasco." She said the name of her street,
sang it like a question. Also told
her name, like a gravestone with lovely flowers,
a veto against our stay together.

9

Sitting in a dark café
on Coronel Diaz Street.
Bitter hero, dead.

A small cup of coffee was enough
for an extended stay.
A newspaper in a language I didn't know.

I scattered cake crumbs on a plate
as for a bird: you came
eyeing about.

I sit, quiet, see you,
you eat quickly,
fly.

10

We lay
exposed and alike
like two halves of an orange
until the evening
became darker than your voice.

Water can be cried out,
stones not: therefore I return to Jerusalem.
"I'll *miss* you!"
Who taught you
to say a vulgar word like that?

11

Intersection.
Corner of Santa Fe
and Cajau, afternoon, waiting:

Which one of all the shadows is mine?
That's why I raised a hand.
That's why I loved you.

Intersecting streets,
a true cross.

12

Silvia's very much changed: her face
grew longer, but in her eyes black
coal remained, glowing in hope of fire.

I sat with her in a café
called "The Family."
She's proud like young soldiers
after their first battle.

She went through many sorrows,
like those an entire nation goes through
in an extended history
(battles and losses, also victories),
alongside her handsome husband. She still
loves him. He loves her very much.

13

A language sickness.
Swaying drunkenness
in the Chinese restaurant where
they translate from Spanish to Hebrew to English,
and far away from them
to Chinese in red kitchen fires.

How may words are shed on the way
how much blood spilled

how much laughter
how much remains nothing!

14

Closeness to Cordoba: I saw
a Jewish girl
from Poland, from Cordoba in Argentina.

Through her eyes
I go back
to Cordoba in Spain
a long way.

Echoes of eyelids anointed white,
chill and damp tunnels
of pupils
and shadows of long eyelashes
like endless fences.

15

Early in the morning the sun
is taken out from cushions of dark velvet.
Family asset, from generation to generation (ah!),
old candelabrum, gold samovar,
survivors of pillage, rape,
Cossacks, Indians, Missionaries,
Crusaders, Mamelukes
(ah!)

Quickly, get up quickly!
Cologne water with hurried daubing
to the armpits, to the nape,
to between the legs still dreaming.
Quickly, quickly, get outside (ah!).

16

And not for the sake of remembering
you live, but to complete this work
which is yours (nonetheless yours) to complete,
and not for the sake of staying you love
and not for the sake of loving you hurt.

Rash, you are, and rush into tiredness,
impatient like a flight-day from country to country,
bartering good hours of life with blessed
rains, at unknown exchange,
passing to lover to passer-by on Corrientes
Street, the streaming, the streaming.

Vamos, let's go. In other
languages it hurts less. Let's go!
There is an illusion of together
at first; afterward, apart.

17

Mourning ever alert
to what softly happens: light
in the covered mirror, voices
behind the heavy curtain.

Mourning ever alert,
joy loses things, careless.
Things fall from you, unnoticed.
But mourning ever alert.

18

Of this time, with light
through the slats of the blind, a head like
Nefertiti, eyes like Sigmund
Freud—frightened—and a wagon wheel
for a lamp, hanging from the ceiling.
"Like fingernails, I'll trim
this love," and a careful placing
of things on the table: the cup, the book,
the spoon, the salt cellar. All those like a heart
beating slowly. "You're using
me!" (another gloss on love).
"You're thinking along very exact
formulas of a heart broken to well-
defined pieces, like once
a heart broke of love."

19

In the Botanical Garden among names, names,
childhood memory, always look for
a public lavatory or a stand for sticky
sweets. Not to remember names,
to flee, to buy food items
for the last meal.

The shopgirl was frightened by our rush. The wrapping
tore, was changed, tore again.
Paper, boxes, cheese
and fruit rolling knew
of all the helplessness of
keeping together.
"You'll be caught forever
in the rigid grid lines of your city."

20

In this city the sky is always
like a layer of gray plaster;
our lives are healing.
The fracture will close, perhaps.

You may go now. "Go,
go," say the traffic lights. Go,
go in peace.
We deserted each other, we gave it up
so that good people could practice

their goodness on us and not forget their mercy.
Buenos Aires will be a different
city when you're gone. "A city without you," she said,
and went her way.

21

City of Borges and Tzivia,
city of an obelisk that never saw
Egypt, city of Susanna
who had not heard of me,
a space between crying and laughter
without crying and without laughter.

There are houses I
want to live in forever,
as in the Middle Ages
the soul asked to live
in a beautiful and pure body.

City of Eduardo:
I wrote his address down in my notebook,
he also wrote mine down in his.
Most likely we won't meet again.

22

Missa Susanna,
wrath of love and fury of longing.

You set my dreams upon me,
I'll set my voice upon you.
Your thighs red in the fire
and the folds of your dress, dark
in order to recite Kaddish.
Peace upon my soul, peace upon your soul,
amen.

Missa Susanna,
this skinny angel
will not guard me from all evil.
But he makes me feel good
with his big eyes that stay
in place.

Missa Susanna,
the paper is tearing on all sides.
The boy who sold the morning news—
by noon his voice already broke.
Loss of names and their bearers.
My coat is marked inside
and my watch strangles my wrist.

Missa Susanna,
may the clods of the words be sweet
to your lovely mouth. Rest now in peace
on your couch. Remember me,
who was little or much,
remember me in the dim corridors

and the delights that awoke
in the great light.
From sieve to sieve
we fall and diminish
from what place to what place,
amen.

23

Good people that took
me from the plane on a hot night
brought me back to it
after several days, as my blood prepared
to become fuel again for the flight. Same
people, on the same hot night.
But I wasn't the same.

The plane, that sucked burning air
into its engines,
swallowed your love and used it too.

Stopover in Rio,
rent-heart de Janeiro.
Repairable.

24

There's a smell of fresh paint here.
Do not forget, there,

in the closed half of the partly
closed eye, painted
white and forgetting.

A slow count backward
into the darkness dimly lit
with what was.

The room. How lonely and abandoned the Spanish
language was in the room.
Afterward the Hebrew too.

The city that gave me calm
and took it from me.

Ballad in the Streets of Buenos Aires

And a man waits in the streets and meets a woman
Precise and beautiful as the clock inside her room
And sad and white as the wall that holds it

And she does not show him her teeth
And she does not show him her belly
But she shows him her time, precise and beautiful

And she lives on the ground floor next to the pipes
And the water which goes up starts at her wall
And he has decided on softness

And she knows the reasons for the weeping
And she knows the reasons for the holding back
And he begins, and he begins to be like her

And his hair grows long and soft like hers
And the hard words of his country melt in her mouth
And his eyes in tears will look like hers

And the traffic lights light up her face
And she is standing there in the allowed and the forbidden
And he has decided on softness

And they walk in the streets which will be in his dreams
And the rain weeps into them as into a pillow
And restless time has made them into prophets

And he will lose her in the Red light
And he will lose her in the Green and in the Yellow
And the light is always there to serve all loss

And he won't be when soap and lotion run out
And won't be when the clock is set again
And won't be when the dress is raveled out in threads

And she will shut his wild letters in a quiet drawer
And lie down to sleep beside the water in the wall
And she will know the reasons for weeping and for holding
	back
And he has decided on softness.

120